German General Rules of Marine Insurance

(ADS)

translated by
Erdewin Pinckernelle
Commercial Judge in Hamburg and former Underwriter

at the request of

Deutscher Transport-Versicherungs-Verband e. V. (DTV)
(The German Marine Insurance Association)

and

Special Conditions for Cargo
(ADS Cargo 1973)
Special Conditions for Open Policies
DTV Strike Riots and Civil Commotions Clauses 1973
DTV Nuclear Energy Clauses 1973
DTV War Clauses 1977
DTV Machinery Clause 1973

4th edition

1977

DE GRUYTER · BERLIN · NEW YORK

CIP-Kurztitelaufnahme der Deutschen Bibliothek

German general rules of marine insurance : (ADS) / transl. by Erdewin Pinckernelle at the request of Dt. Transport-Versicherungs-Verb. e.V. (DTV) (The German Marine Insurance Assoc.). And Special conditions for cargo : (ADS cargo 1973). Special conditions for open policies [u.a.]. - 4. ed. - Berlin, New York : de Gruyter, 1977.
Dt. Ausg. u.d.T.: Allgemeine deutsche Seeversicherungs-Bedingungen.
ISBN 3-11-006879-6

Setting and Printing: Saladruck, 1000 Berlin 36. – Binding: Wübben & Co., 1000 Berlin 42

Preface

The German General Rules of Marine Insurance were drafted by the German Marine Underwriters on consultation with German Chambers of Commerce and other competent Organisations under the leadership of the Hamburg Chamber of Commerce, and published in 1919.

In 1973 Chapter II of Part Two concerning "Cargo Insurance" was replaced after consultation with representatives of the competent Organisations in Trade and Industry as well as with the German Insurance Brokers' Association, by the newly drafted "*Special Conditions for Cargo* (ADS Cargo 1973)", the "*Special Conditions for Open Policies*", and by the DTV Clauses connected with these Special Conditions.

Contents

German General Rules of Marine Insurance

(ADS)

Part One

General Principles

Part Two

Special Rules on the Insurance of Special Subject-Matters

*) Sections 88–99 have been replaced by the "Special Conditions for Cargo Insurance (ADS Cargo 1973)" printed on pages 42 ff., and by the "Special Conditions for Open Policies" printed on pages 51.

Part Three

Special Aggreements (Clauses)

Part Four

Combined Voyages, Law Applicable, Jurisdiction

Other special conditions

Subjects of the rules and special conditions

German general rules of Marine Insurance
(ADS)

Part One: General Principles

Chapter I Insurable Interest

Chapter II Insurable Value, Underinsurance, Overinsurance, Double-insurance

Chapter III Uberrima Fides

Chapter IV Policy, Premium, Forfeit

Chapter XIII Insurance for Account for a Third Party

Part Two: Special Rules on the Insurance of Special Subject-Matters

Chapter I Hull Insurance

Chapter II Cargo Insurance

Chapter III Insurance of Expected Profit and Commission

Chapter IV Insurance of Freight, Ship's Hire, and Passage Money

Chapter V Insurance of Disbursements

Part Three: Special Agreements (Clauses)

Part Four: Combined Voyages, Law Applicable, Jurisdiction

Special Conditions for Cargo Insurance (ADS Cargo 1973)

Special Conditions for Open Policies

Clauses and Other Conditions

DTV Strikes Riots and Civil Commotions Clauses 1973
DTV Nuclear Energy Clauses 1973
DTV War Clauses 1977
DTV Machinery Clause 1973
Instructions to be Followed in Case of Loss or Damage

German General Rules of Marine Insurance (ADS)

Part One

General Principles

Chapter I
Insurable Interest

1. Insurable Interest Defined

(1) Any monetary interest of a person in the safe completion of a marine adventure by a ship or cargo is insurable.

(2) In particular, the following can be the subject-matter of an insurance:

the vessel,
the goods carried,
the profit dependent on the safe arrival at destination of cargo (excepted profit),
the commission dependent on the safe arrival of ship or cargo at destination,
freight,
charter hire,
passage money,
loan on bottomry and respondentia,
disbursements,
other claims secured on the property at stake in a marine adventure,
the risk for which an insurer has given cover (re-insurance).

No insurance of any of the above subject-matters, comprises an insurance of any other. In particular, no insurance is to be deemed a re-insurance unless it is expressly specified as such in the proposal.

(3) In the event of a wrong statement being made in regard to the interest in the insurance, the contract shall not be binding on Underwriters, but they cannot claim an exemption from liability if charter-hire is declared as freight contracted for a certain period of time, or if such freight is declared as charter-hire.

2. No-interest Insurance

(1) In the absence of an insurable interest an insurance contract shall stand void. This applies particularly to gambling policies.

(2) The premium is nevertheless due unless Underwriters when giving cover were aware of the circumstances that made the insurance void.

3. Payment of Premium for No-interest Policies

(1) In the event of para (1) of section 2 the Assured is not liable to pay the premium if at the time when the cover was given, he was unaware, and need not have been aware, of the circumstances that made the cover void. If the insurance is effected by an Agent it is not only the knowledge of the Agent or what he ought to have known but also of the Assured himself that is decisive.

(2) The Assured shall nevertheless pay the premium unless he has informed Underwriters of the circumstances that made the cover void immediately after that fact had come to his knowledge. The same applies when 12 months have elapsed since the conclusion of the contract and the Assured has failed to inform Underwriters of the circumstances within these twelve months.

(3) If the Assured is exempt from the payment of premium, Underwirters are entitled to a fortfeit.

4. Non attachment of Interest, Future Interest

(1) Whenever an interest for which insurance is taken ceases to exist before the beginning of the insurance, or if cover is given for a future interest, and such interest does not materialize, the Assured is not obliged to pay the premium. He remains, however, under that obligation unless, within a period of twelve months, he notifies the insurer of the non-attachment or the non-existence of his interest within that time limit. If the Assured is not liable to pay the premium, Underwriters are entitled to a forfeit.

(2) Once the interest has attached and is covered the Assured remains liable for the premium even if his interest later ceases to exist.

5. Attachment of Risk before Contracting Insurance ("Lost or Not Lost")

(1) An insurance can be contracted for a risk that has attached earlier. Underwriters are not entitled to a premium if, at the time of giving cover, they were aware that loss of or damage to the subject-matter was no longer possible. Underwriters are free of liability for a claim if the Assured, at the time of receiving cover, knew, or ought to have known, that loss of or damage to the subject-matter had already occurred. Underwriters are entitled to the premium provided they had no knowledge of such loss or damage.

(2) Whenever the insurance is effected by an Agent it is not only the knowledge of the Agent or what he ought to have known, but also that of the principal himself that is decisive.

Chapter II
Insurable Value, Underinsurance, Overinsurance, Double-insurance

6. Insurable Value

(1) The insurable value of the interest to be insured is deemed to be equal to its full value.

(2) If by agreement the value of the subject-matter is fixed in terms of a certain amount, such agreed value will take the place of the insurable value. However, Underwriters are entitled to demand a reduction of such agreed value, provided it exceeds the real value of the interest considerably. In the event of the insured sum being lower than the agreed value Underwriters are only liable for such proportion of the measure of indemnity as the amount insured bears to the agreed value, even if the value has been reduced.

(3) A value designated as "provisonally agreed" shall be deemed to be not agreed at all.

7. Separate Valuation

(1) Whenever an insurance contract provides for only one insured amount for various kinds of property, but separate values are agreed for separate objects, such objects shall be deemed, for the benefit of the Assured, as separately insured. This applies particularly to a separately agreed valuation of a specified number of packages (series) within a uniform cargo.

(2) The provision in para (1) shall not apply if it is not possible to identify to which of the various series the goods belong.

(3) The provision in para (1) shall not apply either, even if the series are agreed to be governed by the order in which the packages are bought ashore in a properly executed discharge operation, but the order of their landing is not ascertained by the use of landing numbers or by similar means during discharge or immediately after. It is only by special agreement that series are to be formed and governed by the order in which the individual units are discharged.

8. Underinsurance

If the sum insured is lower than the insurable value, the Assured is deemed to be self-insured for the difference. Underwriters are in such case only liable for such proportion of the loss or damage or expenses as the sum insured bears to the insurable value.

9. Overinsurance

(1) In the event of the sum insured exceeding the insurable value the insurance of the excess shall stand void. The provisions of para (2) of sections 2 and 3 concerning the payment of premium and of a forfeit shall apply.

(2) An insurance contracted fraudulently by the Assured for the purpose of drawing a profit from the overinsurance shall stand void as a whole. Underwriters are all the same entitled to the premium unless at the time of contracting they were aware of the circumstances that would make the contract void.

10. Underwriters' Liability in Case of Double-insurance

(1) In the event of an interest being covered against the same risk by more than one Underwriter, and the aggregate sums insured exceeding the insurable value, Underwriters shall be jointly liable for the amount insured, each for the amount for which he has given cover, but the Assured has no claim for a higher aggregate amount than the loss he has actually suffered.

(2) Between the Underwriters the indemnity to be paid shall be apportioned in the proportion of their commitment. If any of the insurance-contracts is governed by Foreign law, the respective Underwriter can make a claim on the other Underwriter only, if he, according to the law which governs his policy, would be liable to indemnify the other Underwriter in his turn.

(3) A double-insurance effected fraudulently by the Assured for the purpose of drawing a profit therefrom shall stand void. Underwriters are nevertheless entitled to the whole premium unless at the time of contracting they were aware of the circumstances that would make the contract void.

11. Remedy of a Double-insurance

(1) In the event of the Assured having effected the contract that constitutes a double-insurance without having been aware of the existence of the other cover, and the risk in question not having attached, he is entitled to demand both Underwriters to reduce the sum insured and, accordingly, the premium. The reduction shall be made in the proportion of the original commitments of either Underwriter. The Assured shall lose this right if he fails to assert his right immediately after the existence of the double-insurance has come to his knowledge.

(2) If the premium is reduced Underwriters are entitled to a forfeit for the difference.

12. Notice of Double-insurance

The Assured shall notify Underwriters of any existing double-insurance as soon as he becomes aware thereof.

Chapter III
Uberrima Fides

13. All parties concerned shall act in the utmost good faith.

Chapter IV
Policy, Premium, Forfeit

14. The Policy

(1) Upon request of the Assured, Underwriters shall issue to him a policy, i.e. a duly signed document which embodies the insurance contract.

(2) Where a policy has been issued Underwriters are liable for payment only against surrender of that document. A payment made to the bearer shall discharge them.

(3) In case the policy has gone astray or has been destroyed Underwriters shall be liable for payment only after the policy has been invalidated by a Court of Law or after a security other than a guarantee has been tendered. The same applies to Underwriters' obligation to issue a new document. The cost of the latter shall be met by the Assured.

15. Contents of the Policy

The terms of the policy shall be deemed as being approved by the Assured unless he has queried them immediately after the surrender of the document to him, but the legal right of the Assured to plead error or mistake shall not be prejudiced.

16. Premium and Fees Falling Due, Securities Required

(1) The Assured shall pay the premium and the fees forthwith after conclusion of the contract. In particular premium and fees fall due immediately even though, in accordance with the general custom of trade or within the usual procedure of settlement between Underwriters and the Assured, they are paid at a later date.

(2) No matter whether the insurance contract provides for a certain date of payment or for a respite, Underwriters shall be entitled to call for the payment immediately upon the termination of the insurance. However, in the event of the Assured having a claim on Underwriters under the same contract for which he owes the premium, he is allowed to make a set off with such claim, no matter whether or not his claim has fallen due.

(3) If the insurance contract provides for a certain date of payment or for a respite Underwriters are entitled to demand security if and when the solvency of the Assured takes such turn as may prejudice Underwriters' demand for the premium.

17. Overdue Premiums, Failure in Tendering Securities

In case an overdue premium is not paid and no security is tendered upon Underwirters' reminder or call after the expiry of a reasonable time limit set in such reminder or call, the Underwriters shall be exempt from liability provided loss or damage occur before the premium thus called for has been paid or security tendered. Failing the payment of the premium and the tendering of the security Underwriters are also entitled to cancel the insurance without notice. In such case they are entitled to the whole premium for a voyage policy and to a forfeit for a time policy.

18. Forfeit

Any forfeit to be paid to, or withheld by, Underwriters shall amount to half the premium or $^1/_8$ per cent of the sum insured, whichever is lower.

Chapter V
Disclosure, Representation of Risks, Alteration of Risks

19. Disclosure

(1) Before the conclusion of the insurance contract the Assured shall disclose to Underwiters every circumstance known to him and material for the decision to give cover, unless the circumstances are common knowledge. In particular, he shall pass on to Underwriters any information received which is material for the cover, no matter whether or not he holds them to be unfounded or unreliable.

(2) Such circumstances as may come to the knowledge of the Assured before the acceptance of his proposal by Underwriters must be imparted to him as speedily as is feasible in

the ordinary course of business, but must at any rate be transmitted in the same or a similar way as was the proposal.

20. Concealment, Misrepresentation

(1) Unless otherwise provided a failure to disclose a material circumstance, or a misrepresentation of the same, in contravention of section 19 shall discharge Underwriters from liability. The same applies to a failure to disclose a material circumstance because the Assured was not aware of it and his ignorance was due to gross negligence.

(2) Underwriters remain liable if they were aware of the concealed circumstances or of the misrepresentation. The same applies if the disclosure was not made, but the Assured was not at fault.

(3) Where Underwriters remain liable within the meaning of the last sentence of para (2) of this section they are entitled to a higher premium rate (i. e. an additional premium) in accordance with the greater risk.

21. Material Circumstances

Circumstances are deemed to be material particularly if they were misrepresented by the Assured, and he had declared his statement to be correct; furthermore such circumstances as were wilfully concealed or wilfully misrepresented; finally, as a rule, circumstances expressly inquired into by Underwriters.

22. Duty of an Agent to Disclose

In case of an insurance being effected by an Agent of the Assured it is not the knowledge of the Agent, or what he ought to have known, that is decisive for the discharge of Underwriters from liability, but also that of the Principal.

23. Alteration of Risk

(1) After the insurance is contracted the Assured must not alter or, in particular, increase the risk without Underwriters' consent, nor must he suffer the risk to be altered by a third party.

(2) Especially there is an alteration of risk

1. where the beginning or the end of the insured voyage is considerably delayed;
2. where a deviation is made from the declared or customary course of the voyage, though a slight deviation shall be permissable;
3. where the vessel calls on ports other than declared, or calls on them in an order different from what was originally declared or customary; a call for orders being, however, permissible if in general usage for that purpose.

(3) A change of destination form the one declared shall also be deemed to be an alteration of risk.

24. Legal Consequences of an Alteration of Risk

(1) In the event of a violation of the provisions of section 23, and of loss or damage occurring thereafter, Underwriters shall be discharged from liability. The same provision applies where the risk has attached before cover was given, and the Assured has altered the

risk or suffered it to be altered by a third party subsequent to the attachment; without prejudice, however, to the duty of the Assured to disclosure.

(2) Underwriters' liability remains if the alteration was made in the interest of Underwriters or if it was caused by a peril insured against, or if it was imperative for humanitarian reasons, or if the alteration of the risk could not have an influence upon the occurrence of loss or damage, or upon the measure of indemnity.

25. Additional Premium for Alteration of Risks

Provided Underwriters are not discharged from liability by an alteration of risk they are entitled to an additional premium unless the increase of risk was caused by a peril covered by them.

26. Disclosure of Increased Risks

Any increase of risk must be disclosed to Underwriters by the Assured as soon as the latter becomes aware of it, unless the insurer be discharged from liability by the increase.

27. Nondisclosure of Alteration of Risk Relating to Part of the Subject-matter

Where a nondisclosure, misrepresentation, or an alteration of risk concerns only part of the subject-matter and discharges Underwriters in so far from liability they can only avoid the insurance for the remaining part, if it must be assumed that in the then existing circumstances they would not have given cover for such part alone. If they can and do avoid the insurance the Assured is not liable for the respective premium but only for the forfeit Underwriters may claim.

Chapter VI
Insured Perils, Duration of Cover

28. Insured and Uninsured Perils

Unless otherwise provided the insurance covers any peril to which the vessel or the cargo is exposed during the continuance of the cover. Underwriters are, in particular, liable for loss or damage caused by penetration of seawater, collision of ships, stranding, shipwreck, fire, explosion, lightning, earthquake, ice, or caused by theft and pilferage, piracy, looting, or any other acts of violence, but Underwriters are only liable within the limits of these Rules and in no way for a maritime lien, or for loss or damage caused by a delay of the voyage.

29. General Average

(1) Underwriters are liable for any general average contributions to be made by the Assured as well as for any sacrifice of the matter insured in general average. The Assured may also call upon Underwriters to guarantee his contributions, but Underwriters are only liable in so far as the general average measure was taken in order to prevent a peril covered by them.

(2) Where only such cargo is shipped as belongs to the shipowner, the sacrifices which would be a general average act if the goods were owned by someone else, shall be deemed to be general average losses.

30. General Average Contributions

(1) Underwriters' liability for contributions is governed by the statement of general average. In the case dealt with in para (2) of section 29 the above provision shall not apply, and the liability shall be determined by the York-Antwerp-Rules with the exception of section 18 thereof.

(2) The general average statement shall be drawn up by a person competent in accordance with the law or with local custom.

(3) The statement is to be drawn up at the place of destination or, if that place is not reached, at the place where the voyage ends. If at the latter place no person qualified in accordance with para (2) is available, a competent person available at the nearest place shall be called upon. This provision shall not override a previously made agreement of the parties to another place of adjustment.

(4) The general average statement shall be drawn up according to the Rules which are applicable at the place where it is made, unless the parties have in advance agreed upon the rules of the port of registration of the vessel or upon the York-Antwerp-Rules. Expenses incurred by the fire insurance of cargo discharged at a port of refuge for account of all parties concerned in the general average shall go to the charge of Underwriters, no matter whether the general average rules at the place where the statement is made provide otherwise.

(5) The Assured shall safeguard the interest of Underwriters in the drawing up of the statement. In particular, the expenses of the Assured incurred in the settlement between the other parties to the general average shall only be met by Underwriters in so far as they were necessary.

(6) The statement is binding even if in the drawing up any provisions were wrongly applied or if the statement contains actual mistakes, unless the Assured can be called to account for such misapplication or mistakes.

(7) In so far as Underwriters have indemnified the Assured he is subrogated to the latter's claim on any party to the general average that may have resulted from a mistake in the statement. The provisions in sections 45 and 46 shall apply to the subrogation accordingly.

(8) In the event of the contributory value being higher than the insured value, Underwriters are only liable for the contribution proportionally.

31. Sacrifices

(1) Underwriters are liable for a sacrifice of the insured subject-matter in accordance with the provisions concerning his liability in a case of particular average.

(2) Underwriters are subrogated to the Assured's claim to having his loss made good in general average as soon as such claim arises, but Underwriters shall surrender to the Assured any such part of the indemnity received in general average as exceeds the claim he has paid to the Assured plus the expenses he has made for the collection. In all other respects the provisions of sections 45 and 46 shall apply anologously.

32. General Average Expenses

(1) Underwriters are liable for

1. such expenses incurred by the Assured at the time of the occurrence for the purpose of averting or minimizing loss or damage as he could deem imperative;
2. such expenses as the Assured made at the time of the occurrence upon the request of Underwriters;
3. the cost of ascertaining and assessing loss or damage for which Underwriters are liable, provided and in so far as these could be deemed imperative in the circumstances; Underwriters are not liable, however, for fees paid to experts and advisers or to other persons unless the employment of such persons was agreed in the insurance contract or requested by Underwriters.

(2) The expenses dealt with under numbers 1. and 2. of para (1) shall be met by Underwriters even if they have proved unsuccessful; if requested by the Assured, Underwriters shall advance the amount involved. Where part of the insurable value has remained uninsured or where there is disagreement as to whether or not the measures taken upon request of Underwriters to avert or minimize loss or damage appeared imperative, Underwriters shall advance the amount of the expenses also for such part as will go to the charge of the Assured, Underwriters being liable for all expenses made upon their request even if they do not deem the measures taken upon their request as imperative, and if they remained unsuccessful.

33. Faults of the Assured

(1) Underwriters are discharged from liability if loss or damage is caused wilfully or negligently by the Assured, but must make good the loss or damage due to mistakes in navigation (nautical error) unless the Assured is to blame for a wilful act or gross negligence; the term "nautical error" does not comprise, however, mistakes made in the reception, stowage, safe-keeping, or surrender of cargo.

(2) In cargo insurance Underwriters are not liable either for loss or damage due to wilful or negligent acts committed by the shipper or the consignee.

(3) The Assured cannot be called to answer for acts or ommissions committed by the vessel's crew.

34. Free of Average under Three Percent

(1) Underwriters are not liable for loss or damage under three percent of the insurable value.

(2) Underwriters are liable for contributions in general average and for sacrifices even if they do not amount to three percent of the insurable value. They shall also meet the liability of the Assured to third parties in case of a collision between vessels and their expenses within the meaning of numbers 1. and 2. of para (1) of section 32 and of para (3) of section 95. Losses or expenses for which Underwriters are answerable without the limitation contained in para (1) and the expenses defined in number 3. of para (1) of section 32 shall not be added to the actual damage in the ascertainment as to whether or not the three percent limit is reached.

(3) In hull insurance the aggregate damage during any one voyage must have reached the three percent limit in order to be claimable. "One voyage" within the meaning of this provision is defined as a voyage for which the vessel is re-equipped, or on which the vessels sails under a new charter or contract of affreightment, or after all her cargo has been discharged, as well as any preliminary passage in ballast to the port of loading. The period between two voyages shall be deemed to belong to the past voyage.

35. Free from War Risk)*

(1) Underwriters are not liable for war risks. They are, in particular, not liable for loss or damage caused by warlike measures taken by a belligerent power, no matter whether such power has been recognized as such or not, including, especially, for claims arising from the subject-matter insured being stopped, captured, taken, detained, requisitioned, put under restraint, or being destroyed or damaged by mines layed for belligerent purposes, or through other measures; a measure shall also be deemed as taken by a belligerent power if it has been the measure of a power who joins in the war within six months after the measure has been taken.

(2) In hull insurance Underwirters shall be discharged from liability if the vessel, due to the danger of war, does not sail or continue the voyage, or calls at a port, unless the Assured declares to Underwriters, as soon as an event of this kind comes to his knowledge, his intention to continue the insurance.

(3) In cargo insurance, Underwriters are discharged from liability if goods are unloaded due to the danger of war, unless the Assured, as soon as the unloading, impending or carried out, has been brought to his knowledge, declares to Underwriters forthwith his intention to continue the insurance. In the event of the delay lasting longer than two months Underwriters are liable for subsequent damage or leakage only in the case of stranding, notwithstanding their liability for other occurrences. The provisions of paras (1) and (3) of section 114 concerning Underwriters' liability in a case of stranding shall apply.

(4) In the event of an alteration of the risk which is covered, the alteration being due to dangers of war, Underwriters are entitled to an additional premium unless they are discharged from liability. This applies particularly where a vessel due to the danger of war does not sail or continue the voyage, or calls at a port.

36. Loss Inflicted by Legal Procedure

Underwriters are not liable for losses caused by legal decisions or by the enforcement thereof unless they are liable under the insurance terms for the claim against the Assured which was the object of the legal procedure.

37. Measure of Indemnity

(1) Underwriters are liable for loss or damage suffered during the insured voyage only

*) In cargo insurance para (1) of section 35 is applicable in the wording of the War Risk Exclusion Clause (number 1.1.2.1 of the Special Conditions for Cargo (ADS Cargo 1973). vide page 42.

up to the amount insured. As far as hull insurance is concerned the provisions of para (3) of section 34 are applicable analogously.

(2) Expenses which are to be met by Underwriters in accordance with the provisions of section 32 shall be borne by them no matter whether such expenses added to the otherwise due indemnity proper would exceed the sum insured.

(3) In the event of expenses having arisen from the averting or minimizing, ascertaining or assessment of a claim, or from the reconditioning or repairing of goods damaged in an event insured, as well as contributions in general average having been made, or in the event of the Assured having become liable to meet such expenses or contributions personally, Underwriters shall be liable also for a claim for subsequent loss or damage notwithstanding that expenses or contributions were or are to be made good by them.

(4) In so far as the indemnity and expenses or contributions exceed the amount insured because the Assured must meet the claim of a third party which is due to a collision, the provisons in paras (2) and (3) shall not apply.

38. Discharge from Liability by Payment of Amount Insured

(1) Underwriters are entitled, once loss or damage has occurred, to free themselves of any further liability by paying the sum insured.

(2) In spite of having freed themselves by paying the sum insured, Underwriters remain liable to meet the expenses made by the Assured in averting or minimizing the claim or by the reconditioning or repair of the subject-matter insured before the Assured has received Underwriters' declaration that they intend to free themselves of liability by the payment. The above expenses include the cost for which the Assured is personally liable. The provisions of para (4) of section 37 shall apply.

(3) Underwriters forfeit their right to discharge themselves by paying the amount insured dealt with in the first sentence of para (2) if notice thereof is not served on the Assured within five working-days after Underwriters have become aware of the occurrence and its immediate consequences.

(4) The payment shall not entitle Underwriters to any claim on the subject-matter insured.

39. Time Insurance

If the insurance is contracted for days, weeks, or months, or for a period of several months, the insurance shall commence and terminate at noon of the days agreed for the beginning and the end. Local time at the place or position of the vessel shall apply.

Chapter VII
Information of Underwriters, Averting Losses

40. Information in case of Accident

The Assured shall inform Underwriters without delay of any claimable loss or damage, as well as of any accident to ship or cargo, no matter whether or not such event may result in a claim, provided the accident affects Underwriter's risk materially.

41. Averting or Minimizing Loss or Damage

(1) In case of an occurrence insured the Assured is bound to exert himself as far as feasible to avert or minimize loss or damage. He shall follow the instructions given by Underwriters and, circumstances permitting, call for such instructions. If more than one Underwirter is involved and if their instructions are contradictory the Assured shall act on his own judgement.

(2) The Assured shall follow Underwriters' instructions also in the case of only part of the insurable value being covered. This provision shall not apply if more than half of the insurable value remained uninsured, but in such case sentence 2 of para (2) of section 32 concerning the liability for expenses and advances shall not apply.

(3) Underwriters are not liable for a claim in so far as it is due to the non-compliance with the provisions concerning the averting and minimizing loss or damage unless there was no fault or negligence on the part of the Assured.

Chapter VIII
Submission of Claims, Information, Claims Falling Due

42. Submission of Claims

(1) The Assured shall submit to Underwriters any rightful claim in a written notice not later than 15 months from the termination of the insurance or, in case of a missing vessel, not later than 15 months from the date on which an overdue vessel is presumed to be lost in accordance with para (1) of section 72. The notice shall be deemed to be served within the limit of prescription if it has been dispatched within that time limit.

(2) The claim of the Assured shall be time-barred if the notice is not served in due time in accordance with para (1) of this section.

(3) The above provisions shall not apply to a claim for general average contributions made or to be made by the Assured.

43. Information

After an accident Underwriters may require the Assured to give any information on the circumstances of the occurrence for the ascertainment of the measure of their liability. Documentary evidence may also be requested within reason. Underwriters may also call for a sea-protest provided they have a legitimate interest in it.

44. Claims Account, Settlement Falling Due

(1) The Assured is entitled to a settlement of his claim not before one month has elapsed since he has produced a claims account and submitted the required documentary evidence. If he cannot be called to account for a delay in complying with his obligations within one month the Assured may call for an advance payment of three quarters of the minimum sum the claim is likely to amount to in the circumstances.

(2) The claims account must contain a fair statement of the amounts to be paid by Underwriters for each separate loss and expense. If requested by Underwriters a particular average claim must be submitted in form of a statement drawn up by a person entitled by law or by local custom at the place where the claim is payable.

Chapter IX
Subrogation and Minimizing Claims

45. Subrogation

(1) In the event of the Assured being entitled to claim damages from a third party such right shall pass to Underwriters in so far as they have indemnified the Assured for his loss. The Assured must furnish Underwriters with all information necessary for the prosecution of the claim and surrender all documentary evidence in his possession, as well as furnish Underwriters upon request and at their expense with a duly legalized document embodying evidence of the cession of the claim.

(2) If the Assured waives a claim he has on a third party or if he fails to make use of a title securing his rights and remedies, Underwriters are discharged from liability in so far as they would have been able to make a recovery on the grounds of the rights and remedies ceded to him.

46. Minimizing Claims after Subrogation

The subrogation of Underwriters shall not relieve the Assured of his duty to minimize the claim, especially by withholding the freight. As soon as he gets any information that may be material with regard to the enforcement of a claim on a third party, he shall bring such information forthwith to Underwriters' knowledge and, if required to do so, he shall assist them in the prosecution of the claim and, in particular, take legal action in his own name. The expenses are to be borne by Underwriters and advanced upon request.

Chapter X
Insolvency of Underwriters

47.

In the event of an Underwriter becoming insolvent the Assured is entitled to avoid the contract. He can insure his interest elsewhere at the expense of the insolvent Underwriter, but the Underwriter may avert this by tendering security.

Chapter XI
Prescription

48.

All claims under an insurance contract become timebarred after 5 years. The period of prescription begins at the end of the year in which the insurance expired or during which the loss of an overdue vessel is presumed in accordance with section 72.

Chapter XII
Assignment of Interest, Mortgage of Claims

49. Assignment in General

(1) Where the subject-matter insured is assigned, the assignee for the time of his owner-

ship takes the place of the assignor with regard to all the Assured's rights and duties under the insurance contract, the assignor remaining liable for the premium conjointly with the assignee. Where, however, a cargo policy is assigned the assignee does not become liable for the premium and fees; nor can Underwriters claim, in accordance with section 17, their discharge from liability on account of the premium not having been paid and no security tendered unless, however, the assignee was not in good faith.

(2) The assignment becomes binding on Underwriters with regard to their rights and duties under the insurance contract not before the assignment is brought to their knowledge. The provisions of Articles 406 to 408 of the German Civil Code*) shall apply accordingly. Where, however, a policy was issued for a cargo insurance the above provisions shall not apply for the benefit of Underwriters, unless the assignee was not in good faith.

(3) Underwriters are not liable for loss or damage which would not have occurred without the assignment of the subject-matter having been made, but this provision is not applicable to a sale of merchandise unles the sale was made in wartime and the buyer was a National of a belligerent power.

(4) The assignee is entitled to cancel the insurance without notice. The cancellation must be declared within one month after the assignment or, if the assignee was not aware of the existence of the insurance, within one month after he became aware thereof. If he cancels the insurance he is not liable for the premium.

(5) In case of a forced sale of the subject-matter the provisions in paras (1) to (3) shall likewise apply

*) Article 406: The debtor may also set off against the assignee an existing claim which he has against the assignor, unless he had knowledge of the assignment at the time of the acquisition of the claim, or unless the claim did not become due until after he had acquired such knowledge and after the falling due of the assigned claim.
Article 407: An act of performance by the debtor in favour of the assignor after the assignment, or a juristic act entered into between the debtor and the assignor in respect of the claim after the assignment, is valid as against the assignee, unless the debtor knew of the assignment at the time of performance or of the entering into the juristic act.
If in an action between the debtor and the assignor subsequent to the assignment, a non-appellable judgment relating to the claim has been delivered, the judgment is valid as against the assignee, unless the debtor knew of the assignment at the date when the action was first commenced.
Article 408: If an assigned claim be re-assigned by the assignor to a third party, and if the debtor effects the performance in favour of such third party, or if a juristic act is entered into or an action is commenced between the debtor and such third party, the provisions in Article 407 shall apply "mutatis mutandis" in favour of the debtor as against the former assignee.
The same applies if the assigned claim is re-assigned to a third party by judicial order, or if the assignor makes acknowledgement to the third party that the assigned claim is transferred to the third party by operation of law.

50. Assignment of Ships and Shares in Ships

(1) The provisions of section 49 shall apply analogously to an assignment or a transfer of a share in a ship.

(2) In case of a transfer of an insured vessel the insurance shall terminate; Underwriters are entitled only to one fifth of the pro rata premium for the period between the transfer and the originally agreed termination of the policy. If the vessel is transferred whilst on a voyage the insurance terminates not before the moment in which the insurance would terminate at the next port of destination as provided by sections 66 to 68.

51. Mortgagee of Insurance Claims

In so far as an insurance claim is mortgaged the second half of the second sentence in para (1) of section 49 shall apply in favour of the mortgagee.

Chapter XIII
Insurance for Account of a Third Party

52. Insurance for the Proposer's Own Account, for Account of a Third Party, for Account of Whom it May Concern

(1) Where it is not evident that the Proposer who effects the insurance has not the intention of contracting the insurance in his own name but for account of a third party (insurance for account of another) the insurance shall be deemed to be contracted for account of the Proposer (insurance for own account).

(2) Where the insurance is contracted for a third party and even if the other person or party is expressly named, it is to be presumed that the Proposer does not act as an Agent but in his own name for another's account.

(3) Where the insurance is contracted for account of "whom it may concern", or if it is evident in another way from the contract that it shall be left open whether the interest of the Proposer or of a third party is to be insured, the provisions concerning insurance for account of a third party shall apply, if it becomes obvious that in fact the insurance covers the interest of a third party.

53. Legal Position of the Assured

(1) The rights embodied in the contract of insurance are vested in the Assured for whose account the insurance was contracted. The policy, however, shall only be surrendered to the Proposer who effected the insurance.

(2) The Assured for whose account the insurance was contracted cannot make a claim under the insurance or enter into legal proceedings unless he is in possession of a policy or unless the proposer agrees.

54. Legal Position of the Proposer

(1) The Proposer who effected the insurance can in his own name exercise the assured's rights embodied in the contract.

(2) Where a policy has been issued, the Proposer is only entitled to receive payments or to assign the rights of the Assured if he is in possession of the policy or if the Assured has given his approval.

(3) Underwriters are only liable to make payments to the Proposer if the latter produces evidence that the Assured has approved of the cover to be taken.

55. Legal Relations between the Proposer and the Assured

The Proposer who effected the insurance is not bound to surrender the policy to the Assured or, in case of bankruptcy of the latter, to the receiver before he has been satisfied for claims he has on the Assured with regard to the subject-matter insured. He is entitled to satisfay himself for such claims out of the insurance claims against Underwriters or out of the collected indemnity. He enjoys priority over the Assured and his creditors.

56. Compensation

Underwriters may set off any claim they have on the Proposer who effected the insurance against an insurance claim in so far as their claim results from the insurance taken by the Proposer for the Assured.

57. Parties Responsible for Disclosure and Representation

(1) In the event of nondisclosure or misrepresentation of material facts the legal consequences shall depend on what was known or ought to have been known not only to the Proposer who effected the insurance but also to the Assured; the same applies to the exemption of the Proposer from his liability for the premium, where the interest has not attached.

The plea of no fault can only be made if the material fact to be disclosed was known or ought to have been known neither to the Proposer nor to the Assured.

(2) Where a cover is given on a "lost or not lost" basis, Underwriters are discharged from liability if the Proposer or the Assured at the time the cover was given knew or ought to have known that loss or damage had already occurred.

(3) Where the insurance was effected without the knowledge of the Assured, it shall be of no avail whether or not he knew or ought to have known of the occurrence. The same applies if a notification of the Proposer was not feasable in due time. Such notification shall be deemed not to have been made in due time if it was not made as speedily as was feasable in the ordinary course of business and if it was not made at least in the same or a similar way in which the order to conclude the contract was given.

(4) The Proposer cannot plead that the contract was effected without the knowledge of the Assured unless at the time of contracting he had disclosed that fact to Underwriters.

Part Two
Special Rules on the Insurance of Special Subject-Matters

Chapter I
Hull Insurance

58. Seaworthiness

(1) Underwriters are not liable for loss or damage resulting from the vessel having put to sea in a state of unseaworthiness or from her not having been properly equipped, manned, or loaded, or without the certificates necessary for the vessel, the crew, or her cargo.

If loss or damage occurs prior to the sailing Unterwriters are not liable if the occurence was due to the vessel being unfit for service in port.

(2) In the event of the vessel being lost or damaged without there being any external event and there being doubt about the causes, the occurrence shall be deemed to have been caused by the circumstances explained in para (1).

59. Wear and Tear, Age

Underwriters are not liable for loss or damage caused solely by wear and tear of the vessel within her normal service, or by her age, by rot, rust, or worms. The following shall be deemed to be loss and damage due to wear and tear in the ordinary service: loss or tearing of sails, or other damage to same, even if caused by carrying press; damage to anchors, ropes, chains, or to the rigging; the cutting away of ropes or sails on account of such damage; the cutting away or slipping of anchors, anchor chains, or cables.

The following shall not be deemed to be loss or damage due to wear and tear: damage to sails due to the catching of heavy seas; breakage of spars, and any damage to lashed sails in an accident.

60. Dangerous Cargo

(1) Underwriters shall not be liable for loss or damage resulting from the carriage of such explosives or goods susceptible to spontaneous combustion as, by the Rules of the German States bordering the Sea concerning the Carriage of Dangerous Goods by Merchant Vessels, are precluded from the carriage; nor shall they be liable for loss or damage caused by such goods as are admitted to carriage on merchant vessels under certain precautions, and the rules governing such precautions were violated; in case of a shipment from a Foreign port where there are local rules for the carriage of dangerous goods by merchant vessels these rules shall be applicable. Underwriters remain liable, however, if the Assured did not know or need not have known of either the shipment, or the enfringement of the said rules. If Underwriters remain liable they are entitled to an additional premium.

(2) Underwriters are not liable for loss or damage resulting from the vessel being loaded on the insured voyage for more than one-third of her loading capacity with bone-ash, chalk, charcoal, clay, waste of clay, cement, coal, earth, fertilizer, hay, grain and other agricultural produce shipped in bulk, as well as bulk cargo in general, iron and steel (including rails and girders), lime, minerals (including marble, slate, stones, or tiles), ore, and salt. The provisions of sentences 2 and 3 of para (1) apply.

61. Forcing Standing Ice

Underwriters are not liable for loss or damage caused by an attempt to force the vessel through standing ice unless such attempt was imperative in order to avert or minimize loss or damage if covered by them.

62. Jettison of Deck Cargo

Underwriters are not liable for general average contributions in so far as they were occasioned by jettison of deck cargo.

63. Sacrifices whilst Sailing in Ballast

Whilst a vessel sails or is to sail in ballast, Underwriters are not liable for sacrifices which would be considered as general average sacrifices if the vessel had sailed or were to sail with cargo. Underwriters cannot claim discharge from liability if they were notified of the proposed ballast journey when the insurance was proposed.

64. Assistance given by the Vessel to Third Parties

Underwriters are not liable for loss or damage suffered by the insured vessel whilst being used as lighter or whilst towing other vessels or rendering assistance in so far as the consideration received for such assistance was meant to cover such loss or damage.

65. Damage to Cabins or Machinery

Underwriters are not liable for damage to cabin equipment and effects unless the vessel be stranded. The same applies to Underwriters' liability for damage to machinery. This includes particularly the main engine (with the auxiliary machinery and installations necessary for the operation of the engine, as well as the boilers and their installation with the funnel, shaft, propeller and wheel), the machinery on deck, steering gear with the stearing engine and chains as far as the quadrant, pumps for the vessel's use, electric light installation, the wireless equipment, and the refrigerating plant. The provisions of para (1) and (2) of section 114 below shall apply.

66. Duration of Cover

(1) In a voyage policy the cover commences at the beginning of the loading operation of cargo or ballast or, if neither cargo nor ballast is taken, at the time when the vessel sails. The cover terminates as soon as the discharge operation of cargo or ballast at destination has come to an end or, if neither cargo nor ballast is discharged, as soon as the vessel has dropped anchor or has been moored at her proper place. In case the discharge of the vessel is unduly delayed by the Assured the cover shall terminate at the time when the discharge operation would have been completed without such delay.

(2) If prior to the completion of the discharge cargo or ballast is taken for a new voyage, the cover terminates as soon as the new loading begins.

(3) If after the commencement of the cover the insured voyage is abandoned, the cover terminates at the place where the voyage is abandoned, and the rules set for the termination at destination shall apply accordingly.

67. Continuation of Cover under a Voyage Policy

(1) In the event of the vessel arriving at destination in a damaged condition, and Underwriters being liable for the damage, the cover shall remain in force until the completion of the repair. If repair is unduly delayed by the Assured the cover shall terminate at the time when the repair would have been completed without such delay. The Assured can renounce the continuation by notifying Underwriters of his renunciation, immediately after having become aware of the damage. If the cover is continued Underwriters are entitled to an additional premium in consideration of the longer duration of the cover.

(2) The provisions of para (1) shall not apply if repair is only possible at a place other than the destination, and if it has not been ascertained in accordance with section 74 that the vessel is fit to proceed to the place of repair.

68. Continuation of Cover under a Time Policy

Where under a time policy the vessel on the stipulated expiry of the insurance is at sea the cover shall continue until the time when the cover would end, in accordance with sections 66 and 67, at the next port of destination. The Assured can renounce the continuation by notifying Underwriters of his renunciation before the vessel has sailed. If the cover is continued Underwriters are entitled to an additional premium in consideration of the longer duration of the voyage; if the vessel is missing, they are entitled to the premium until the vessel is presumed lost according to section 72 below.

69. Insurance of Successive Voyages

If insurance is taken for a number of successive voyages the cover includes the time between the voyages.

70. Insurable Value

(1) The insurable value is deemed to be equal to the value of the vessel at the time of the commencement of the insurance. Such value shall not include the cost of equipment, wages and pay for the crew, and insurance charges.

(2) This value shall also be deemed to be the insurable value at the time when loss or damage occurs.

71. Total Loss

(1) A total loss entitles the Assured to the amount insured. The value of any salvage and recovery as well as any indemnification received from third parties shall be deducted before settlement. The value of salvage shall be determined by public auction if requested by Underwriters.

(2) The vessel shall also be deemed to be a total loss if the Assured is irretrievably deprived of it, in particular if the vessel be sunk and no salvage possible, or if the vessel be so damaged as to cease to be a thing of the kind insured.

(3) By the settlement of the claim Underwriters are subrogated to all rights and remedies of the Assured in respect of the vessel. The Assured must furnish Underwriters with any information necessary for the prosecution of the claim and surrender all documentary evidence in his possession as well as furnish Underwriters upon request and at their expense with a legalized document containing evidence of the cession of his rights and remedies.

(4) The subrogation of Underwriters shall not free the Assured from his duty to minimize the claim in so far as Underwriters are unable to do so themselves. As soon as he gets any information that may be material for a prosecution of a claim on a third party, he shall bring such information forthwith to Underwriters' knowledge and, if requested to do so, assist them in the recovery and realization of any salvage of the vessel. The costs are to be met and, upon request, advanced by Underwriters.

72. Missing Vessel

(1) The Assured is also entitled to call for the payment of the sum insured if the vessel is missing and must be considered lost. The vessel is lost if she has not reached the next port of call or distination within a certain lapse of time and no news of her has been received. The time lapse for the presumption of an actual loss shall be thrice the time the vessel would require in normal circumstances to cover the distance from the position from where the last news was received, to the next port of call or destination, but at least two months if the vessel is power driven or three months if she is a sailing vessel. In war-time when the receipt of news may be delayed, the time limit shall be six months in either case.

(2) The call for settlement cannot be made conditionally or subject to a time limit.

(3) By the call for settlement Underwriters are subrogated to the rights and remedies of the Assured in respect of the vessel (abandonment). The provisons of the second sentence in para (3) and of para (4) of section 71 relating to the assistance to be given to Underwriters shall apply.

(4) The Assured is debarred from exercising the right conceded to him in the first sentence in para (1) if news is received from the vessel before he made the call for payment.

73. Seizure and Detention by Authorities, Piracy

The provisions contained in section 72 shall also apply accordingly where a vessel has been seized or detained by Authorities or captured by pirates, with the exception of the provisions for the time limits set therein. In either of the above events the time limit shall be two months.

74. Partial Loss

(1) Any partial loss shall be ascertained by experts.

(2) Both Underwriters and the Assured or, in his place, the shipmaster shall immediately appoint an expert each.

(3) In the event of the experts disagreeing they shall appoint an umpire. The latter may also be appointed prior to the survey. If the experts disagree on the umpire to be called upon, they must both nominate an umpire, and lots shall be drawn. If the vessel is in a Foreign port, and agreement cannot be reached, the Assured or the master shall request the consul of the country where the vessel is registered, to appoint the umpire. In a port where there is no consul of the vessel's nationality, or if the consul is unwilling to meet the request, another consul shall be called, and if he is unwilling, too, a public servant of the country where the vessel lies, who is competent for such appointments, shall be referred to.

(4) In the event of Underwriters failing to nominate their expert although requested to do so, the Assured or the master shall refer the appointment of an expert to the Local Chamber of Commerce. If the vessel lies in a Foreign port the Assured may proceed according to sentences 4 and 5 of para (3) of this section.

(5) The experts shall survey and ascertain the damage and issue a survey report. The interested parties should be present at the inspection if feasable. The report must contain: –

1. the names of the experts and other persons who took part in the survey,
2. the names of the parties or individuals who appointed the experts,

(3) In cargo insurance Underwriters are only liable if the goods insured fail to reach their destination.

(4) Underwriters are liable neither for general average contributions or sacrifices nor for expenses and costs according to section 32 or to section 1.5.1.2 "ADS Cargo 1973" (printed below).

121. "War Risk Only"

(1) Underwriters are only liable for war risk. They are, in particular, liable for loss or damage caused by warlike measures of a belligerent Power, no matter whether such Power be recognized as such or not, including especially for claims arising from the subject-matter insured having been stopped, captured, taken, detained, requisitioned, put under restraint, damaged or destroyed by mines layed for belligerent purposes, or through other measures; a measure shall also be deemed as taken by a belligerent Power if it has been the measure of a Power who joins in the war within six months after the measure has been taken.

(2) The provisions of an insurance which excludes war risk shall apply analogously (vide section 35), but within the terms of paras (3) to (7) of this section as below.

(3) Underwriters are not liable for general average or other expenses incurred because, due to the dangers of war, the vessel does not sail, does not continue the voyage, calls at a port of refuge, or if cargo is discharged, warehoused, or sent on by other conveyances.

(4) Underwriters are not discharged from liability in the cases dealt with in paras (2) and (3) of section 35 above, subject, however, to the limitation of liability provided for in the second sentence of para (3) of section 35 above.

(5) In hull insurance Underwriters are not liable for loss or damage due to the presence of contraband on board the vessel. Underwriters remain liable, however, if the Assured was not or need not be aware of the presence of such cargo. If Underwriters remain liable they are entitled to an additional premium.

(6) The vessel shall be considered a total loss in accordance with para (2) of section 71 above, where a vessel has been condemned a legal prize. The provisions in section 72 above concerning missing vessels shall apply in accordance with section 73 above, especially in the event of a belligerent or other like Power within the meaning of the second sentence of para (1) of this section having stopped, captured, detained, requisitioned, or put the vessel under restraint; the time limit set in the second sentence of section 73 above shall, however, be replaced by a lapse of six months.

(7) In cargo insurance, goods that at the time of the conclusion of the insurance were contraband shall not be deemed as covered by the contract. This applies particularly to open policies. Underwriters remain liable, however, provided the Assured neither knew, or ought to have known, that the goods were contraband. If Underwriters remain liable they are entitled to an additional premium.

122. "Including War Risk"

(1) Underwriters are also liable for war risk.

(2) In the event of Underwriters being discharged from liability for reasons of nondisclosure, misrepresentation, or an alteration of risks, and the above reasons concerning

only the war-risk, then they remain liable for the conventional risks (vide section 35); if the above reasons concern only the conventional risks Underwriters remain liable for war-risk (vide section 121 above), unless it can be reasonably assumed that they would not have given cover for these risks separately.

(3) The provisions in section 121 above apply analogously, but without prejudice to para (4) of section 35 concerning an additional premium for an alteration of the risk if due to dangers of war.

123. "Total Loss Only"

Underwriters are only liable where the subject-matter insured is totally lost or has been missing and must be considered as totally lost within the meaning of section 72, also where it has been seized by authorities or captured by pirates. In hull insurance Underwriters are also liable if the vessel is unfit for, or unworthy of, repair. Underwriters are neither liable for general average contributions and sacrifices, nor for expenses and cost within the terms of section 32 and section 1.5.1.2 of "ADS Cargo 1973". In cargo insurance Underwriters are not liable either for goods being lost owing to damage, or, in particular, for their being destroyed in their original nature.

124. "From Warehouse to Warehouse"

(1) The risk attaches at the time when the goods are removed from the place of their last storage at the place of shipment for conveyance on the insured voyage.

(2) The risk terminates when the goods are delivered at destination to the place determined for storage by the consignees; the cover for loss or damage due to fire, explosion, lightning, or earthquake terminates not later than at midnight of the tenth day after the day of discharge; the same applies to loss or damage caused by other perils, unless the goods were brought to their final destination without delay after their discharge.

(3) These Rules shall apply analogously in so far as goods are conveyed overland or on inland waterways.

Part Four
Combined Voyages; Law Applicable; Jurisdiction

125. Combined Sea and Inland Voyages

Where an insurance covers a voyage that is undertaken both by sea and overland or on inland waters these Rules shall apply to the whole combined voyage accordingly.

126. German Law Applicable

German Law shall apply to the relations between the parties, but Statute Law shall apply to marine insurance only in so far as the statutes are binding and unalterable.

127. Jurisdiction

Difference between the parties to an insurance contract shall be settled exclusively before the court of Underwriters' legal domicile. If, however, the insurance contract was concluded by an Agent at Underwriters' or the Agent's branch office, and such office is domiciled outside the jurisdiction of the court of Underwriters' main domicile, then the contract shall also come under the jurisdiction of the Court of the branch office.

German General Rules of Marine Insurance Special Conditions for Cargo (ADS Cargo 1973)

1 **Extent of cover**

1.1 **Insured and non-insured risks**

1.1.1 The insurance covers all perils to which the goods are exposed during the currency of the insurance.

1.1.2 The insurance does not cover the risks of

1.1.2.1 war, civil war or warlike events, as well as events arising – independent of a state of war – from the hostile use of engines of war and the presence of engines of war as a consequence of one of these risks;

1.1.2.2 strikes, lockouts, labour disturbances, political acts of violence, riots and other civil commotions;

1.1.2.3 nucelar energy;

1.1.2.4 seizure, deprivation or other acts of authorities.

1.1.2.5 For the inclusion of these risks, the respective DTV Clauses shall apply. If these are not attached to the policy, the versions last published in the "Bundesanzeiger" prior to attachment of the insurance shall apply.

1.2 **Forms of cover**

A **Stranding Cover** (where agreed)

The insurance covers, irrespective of percentage, loss of or damage to the goods as a consequence of

a) stranding; there is a case of stranding where the vessel carrying the goods strikes ground or runs aground, capsizes, sinks, founders, collides with other vessels or objects or is damaged by ice;
b) accident to another means of conveyance carrying the goods;
c) collapse of storage buildings;
d) fire, lightning, explosion; earthquake, seaquake, volcanic eruptions and other natural catastrophes; impact or crashing of a flying object, parts thereof or its cargo;
e) jettison, washing overboard or being lost overboard as a result of heavy weather;
f) sacrifice of goods;
g) discharge, intermediate storage and loading of the goods at a port of refuge called at on account of a risk insured against.

The insurance also covers, irrespective of percentage,

the total loss of whole packages, excluding loss arising from damage or disappearance (e. g. theft, embezzlement, non-delivery)

and

total loss of whole packages as a result of damage caused by accidents during loading and unloading of the means of conveyance.

B **Restricted Full Cover** (where agreed)

The insurance covers loss of or damage to the goods as a consequence of a risk insured against, but

a) for loss or damage under 3 % of the insurable value and
b) for loss or damage caused by
   - disappearance (e. g. theft, embezzlement, nondelivery)
   - breakage, bending, denting, scratching, chipping of paint, polish or enamel, tearing of sacks or damage to the packing
   - ship's sweat, rust or oxidation
   - tainting
   - leakage
   - vermin, worms, rats or mice

only to the extent to which such loss or damage is a consequence of one of the occurrences specified under the Stranding Cover.

C **Full Cover** (unless otherwise agreed)

The insurance covers, irrespective of percentage, loss of or damage to the goods insured as a consequence of a risk insured against.

D **Goods in Containers or Barges carried by Ocean-Going Vessels**

(applies only where agreed)

Goods carried in closed containers or in barges carried by ocean-going vessels are insured on deck on the same conditions as in the hold.

1.3 **Special cases**

1.3.1 Deck cargo

For goods loaded on deck with the consent of the Assured, Stranding Cover only shall apply.

1.3.2 Goods transhipped and returned

For goods which, subsequent to a previous voyage, are on-carried or returned on the insured voyage, Stranding Cover only shall apply, unless Underwriters were informed or should have been aware thereof at the time the contract was concluded or the loss or damage sustained could have occured only on the insured voyage.

1.3.3 Damaged Goods

If the goods are already damaged at the time the insured voyage commences, the insurance covers loss or damage only if the damage existing at the time the voyage commences has no influence on the loss or damage occurring during the voyage.

1.4 **Exclusions**

1.4.1 The insurance does not cover loss or damage caused by

1.4.1.1 delay;

1.4.1.2 inherent vice or nature of the goods;

1.4.1.3 ullages or differences in quantity, measure or weight customary in the trade, which are, however, deemed to have been taken into account if a deductible has been agreed;

1.4.1.4 normal atmospheric humidity and ordinary temperature fluctuations;

1.4.1.5 lack or insufficiency of packing customary in trade.

1.4.2 The insurance also excludes indirect loss or damage.

1.5 **Insured expenses and charges**

1.5.1 The insurance covers

1.5.1.1 general average contributions payable by the Assured by virtue of an average statement drawn up according to law or York Antwerp Rules, provided the general average act was performed in order to prevent loss or damage for which Underwriters would be liable. Where the contributory value exceeds the insurable value, Underwriters shall be liable in full up to the amount of the sum insured. The provisions governing under-insurance shall remain unaffected.

1.5.1.2 the costs of transhipment, of temporarily warehousing the goods and the extra costs of forwarding them on account of an insured accident after the risk has attached, if reasonably incurred or incurred at Underwriters' request;

1.5.1.3 expenses incurred in order to avert or minimize loss or damage arising from a risk insured against and charges by third persons for ascertaining the extent of loss or damage, if reasonably incurred or incurred at Underwriters' request.

1.5.2 The Assured may call upon Underwriters to guarantee payment of general average contributions and to advance sufficient funds in order to meet the expenses incurred in averting or minimizing an impending loss covered by the insurance.

2 **Alteration of risk**

2.1 The Assured is entitled to alter and, in particular, to increase the risk or to allow such alteration by a third person.

2.2 If the Assured alters the risk or receives knowledge of any alteration of risk, he is under obligation to notify Underwriters thereof immediately.

2.3 There is an alteration of risk, in particular, where

- there has been a considerable delay in commencing or completing the voyage
- the designated or usual course of the voyage has been considerably departed from
- the port of destination has been changed
- the goods have been lightered where this is locally not customary
- the goods have been loaded on deck.

2.4 Where the Assured has not notified Underwriters of an increase in risk, Underwriters shall be discharged from liability, unless the infringement of the obligation to notify was due to neither wilful intent nor gross negligence, or the increase of risk could in no way have had any influence on the occurrence of loss or damage or the extent thereof.

2.5 In the event of an increase of risk, Underwriters shall be entitled to an additional premium to be agreed, unless such increase in risk is made in furtherance of the interests of Underwriters, for reasons of humanity or is caused by a risk insured against to which the goods are exposed.

3 Means of conveyance

3.1 For carriage by ocean-going vessels, the DTV Classification Clause shall apply.

3.2.1 Transportation by other means of conveyance is insured only if such means of conveyance fulfils the necessary requirements of suitability for the loading and carriage of the goods. Inland waterway vessels are deemed to be suitable if appropriately classified by a recognised classification society.

3.2.2 Where these prerequisites are not present, carriage is insured notwithstanding, provided the Assured has selected the means of conveyance or the forwarding agent or the carrier with the necessary prudence and foresight. If the Assured receives knowledge of unsuitability of the means of conveyance, he is under obligation to notify Underwriters thereof immediately and pay an additional premium to be agreed.

4 Alteration of means of conveyance

4.1 Underwriters are discharged from liability if the goods are carried by a means of conveyance other than that agreed in the contract of insurance, or are transhipped although the contract of insurance stipulates direct transport. The same applies if a specific means of conveyance or a specific route has been agreed.

4.2 The liability of Underwriters remains if, after the risk has attached and as a consequence of a risk insured against, the means of conveyance is altered or the voyage is abandonned without the consent of the Assured. The provisions governing alteration of risk shall apply accordingly.

5 Duration of insurance (warehouse to warehouse)

5.1 The risk attaches when the goods are removed from the place of their last storage at the place of shipment for conveyance on the insured voyage.

5.2 The insurance terminates, according to whichever case shall first occur,

5.2.1 when the goods are delivered at destination to the place designated by the consignee (place of final delivery), or

5.2.2 when the goods, following discharge at the port of destination, are forwarded to a destination not agreed in the contract of insurance and as a result of the change of destination the risk is increased, or

5.2.3 when intermediate storage arranged by the Assured exceeds 30 days, or

5.2.4 upon expiry of 60 days after discharge from the ocean-going vessel at the port of destination;

5.2.5 upon transfer of title when the goods are sold on account of a loss arising from a risk insured against.

6 **Insurable value**

The insurable value of the goods is their ordinary trade value or, if there is no such special value, the common value current at the place of shipment at the time the risk attached, plus the charges for insurance, the expenses incurred up to the time the goods are delivered to the carrier and the freight paid independent of delivery.

7 **Measure of indemnity**

7.1 **Total loss**

In the case of total loss of the goods, or if the Assured is deprived of the goods without hope of recovery or if it is ascertained by experts that the goods have been reduced to such a state as to cease to be a thing of the kind insured, the measure of indemnity shall be that portion of the sum insured accruing to the goods, less the value of salvage.

7.2 **Missing goods**

Where the goods are missing together with the means of conveyance, the measure of indemnity shall be as in the case of total loss, unless a loss must in all probability be presumed as a consequence of a risk not insured against. The means of conveyance is deemed to be missing if from the time of its scheduled arrival 60 days – on European inland waterways 30 days – have elapsed, and up to the time of claim being made no news of it has been received. Where the forwarding of news may have been delayed on account of war, warlike events, civil war or civil commotions, the time from which the goods are presumed lost shall be extended according to circumstances, but to not more than 6 months.

7.3 **Damaged goods**

7.3.1 In the event of the goods or part of the goods being damaged, the ordinary trade value or, if no such value exists, the common price must be ascertained, for which the goods would have sold at the place of destination had they arrived there sound (sound value), and also the value upon arrival in damaged condition. The measure of indemnity is such proportion of the insurable value as the difference between the sound and damaged value bears to the sound value of the goods.

7.3.2 The damaged value can also be ascertained by open sale or public auction if this is requested by Underwriters immediately upon receiving knowledge of the material facts of the extent of damage; in such case, the gross proceeds of the sale replace the damaged value for the purpose of adjustment. If, according to the conditions of sale, the seller has to advance money, Underwriters guarantee the payment of the sales proceeds provided they agreed to the conditions of sale.

7.4 **Reconditioning**

In the event of loss of or damage to parts of the goods, the Assured may request – in lieu of a proportion of the insurable value – indemnification of the cost necessary at the time the loss or damage is ascertained for replacing or reconditioning the lost or damaged parts, such cost, however, being limited to the sum insured and to the proportion which the sum insured bears to the sound value.

7.5 **Machinery and apparatus**
Where machinery, machinery parts and apparatus are insured, the DTV Machinery Clause shall apply.

7.6 **Under-insurance**
If the sum insured is less than the insurable value, Underwriters are liable for loss or damage or expenses incurred for such proportion only of the measure of indemnity as such sum insured bears to the insurable value.

7.7 **Franchise**
Where a franchise is agreed without a modus of calculation being determined, such franchise shall, at the option of the Assured, be calculated on the value of each package (each piece in case of unpacked goods), each lot, each series or each bill of lading or on the value of the whole shipment or the contents of each ship's hold or lighter.

7.8 **Sale of goods prior to termination of voyage**
7.8.1 Where, after the risk has attached and without Underwriters being discharged from liability, the vessel has abandonned her voyage or for any other reason the voyage has not been completed, Underwriters are entitled to request the Assured to sell the goods with their assistance, either by open sale or public auction, if the goods cannot be forwarded within a reasonable time or without incurring unreasonable expense. If the goods must be sold at the request of Underwriters, the sale must take place forthwith.
7.8.2 Where the goods have been sold, the Assured is entitled to claim the difference between the insured value and the proceeds of the sale. This also applies where the goods have to be sold during the course of the voyage on account of an accident arising from perils insured against.
7.8.3 If, according to the conditions of sale, the seller has to advance money, Underwriters guarantee the payment of the sales proceeds provided they agreed to the conditions of sale.

7.9 **Non-acquired interest; costs saved**
Where an insured interest in anticipated profits, additional value, customs duty, freight or other expenses has not been acquired at the time loss or damage occurs, that proportion of the sum insured accruing thereto shall not be taken into account when the claim is assessed. The same shall apply to costs saved in consequence of loss or damage occurring.

7.10 **Indemnity from third parties**
7.10.1 Any sums received by the Assured from third parties on account of the loss or damage sustained shall be deducted from the measure of indemnity.

7.10.2 Where compensation cannot be claimed from third parties entrusted with the carriage of the goods on account of their having exonerated themselves beyond the legal or customary limits, Underwriters shall to such extent be discharged from liability. This shall not apply where the Assured has no influence on such exoneration.

7.11 **Subrogation to rights and remedies**

7.11.1 In the event of the Assured requesting payment of the sum insured, all rights and remedies in and in respect of the insured goods shall pass to Underwriters, upon such payment being made, at their option only. Subrogation shall not ensue if Underwriters do not exercise such option immediately upon receiving knowledge of the circumstances of loss or damage.

7.11.2 The subrogation of Underwriters to the rights and remedies of the Assured shall not relieve the latter from his duty to take all possible measures to minimize the loss or damage, insofar as Underwriters are not able to do so themselves. The Assured must furnish Underwriters with all information necessary for the prosecution of the claim, deliver or issue all documents by which such claim can be established and render every assistance required for recovery of the goods and turning to account whatever remains of them. The costs are be borne by Underwriters; they must, if requested to do so, advance the sums necessary to meet the expenses. That part of the net proceeds of sale exceeding the sum insured shall be refunded to the Assured.

7.11.3 In the event of subrogation not ensuing, the Assured shall refund to Underwriters the common price or the net sale proceeds of goods recovered.

7.11.4 The subrogation of claims against third parties and the right of Underwriters to abandon remain unaffected.

7.12 **Delay**

Underwriters – apart from their liability for interest as provided by law – are liable to the Assured for a loss arising from delay in payment only in the event of their having delayed the payment wilfully or by gross negligence.

8 **Procedure in the event of loss or damage**

8.1.1 In the event of loss or damage occurring, the Assured must follow the instructions of Underwriters, immediately request attendance of the claims agent nominated in the insurance policy or certificate to survey and certify the loss or damage and forward the claim survey report to Underwriters.

8.1.2 Where substantial reasons can be proved, the Assured may call in the nearest Lloyd's Agent, instead of the nominated claims agent, to survey and certify the loss or damage.

8.2 In the event of dispute, either party shall be entitled to request that the cause and extent of loss or damage be ascertained by experts.

8.2.1 In such case, two experts must be immediately appointed, one by each party. Each party shall be entitled to request the other party in writing to appoint the second expert, at the same time advising the other party of the expert nominated by them. In the event of such party failing to nominate its expert within four weeks following receipt of such request, the requesting party shall be entitled to have said expert appointed by the Chamber of Commerce – or by the consular representation of the Federal Republic of Germany – in whose area of jurisdiction the goods are located.

8.2.2 Before entering upon the reference, the two experts shall nominate an umpire. Should the experts fail to agree on an umpire, the umpire shall, upon application by one or both parties, be appointed by the Chamber of Commerce – or the consular represention of the Federal Republic of Germany – in whose area of jurisdiction the goods are located.

8.2.3 The findings of the experts must contain all facts necessary for assessing the cause of the loss or damage and the measure of indemnity of Underwriters.

8.2.4 The experts shall submit their findings to both parties simultaneously. In the event of the experts arriving at divergent findings, Underwriters shall immediately submit said findings to the umpire. The umpire shall then decide on the points at issue within the limits of both experts' findings and shall submit his award to both parties simultaneously.

8.2.5 Each party shall bear the costs of its own expert, the costs of the umpire to be borne by the two parties in equal proportion.

8.2.6 The findings of the experts or the decision of the umpire shall be binding, unless evidence is brought to show that they are obviously inconsistent with the actual material facts.

8.2.7 If the experts or umpire are unwilling or unable to ascertain the loss or damage, or if they are guilty of undue delay, other experts shall be appointed.

8.3 Underwriters may refuse payment until the loss or damage has been ascertained in accordance with the aforegoing provisons. If, due to no fault or negligence of the Assured, the loss or damage has not been ascertained in the manner aforesaid, Underwriters may refuse payment until the loss or damage has been ascertained in some other appropriate manner.

9 Concluding provisions

9.1 Currency

9.1.1 Payments to be made and received shall be effected in the currency of the sum insured.

9.1.2 If, in the event of general average, the contributory value is stated in a currency other than that of the sum insured, such contributory value shall be converted into the currency of the sum insured at the rate of exchange prevailing on the day on which vessel and cargo parted company.

9.2 Insurance for account of another

Where the insurance is concluded for account of another or for account of whom it may concern, the knowledge and conduct of the Assured shall be considered to be equivalent to the knowledge and conduct of the person concluding the insurance.

9.3 **Bailees**

The insurance shall not inure to the benefit of the carrier, baillee, warehouseman or forwarding agent.

9.4 **Coinsurance**

9.4.1 For insurances written by more than one Underwriter, the liability of the individual Underwriters is always a separate and not a joint one, even if the policy or certificate was signed by one Underwriter for and on behalf of all Underwriters.

9.4.2 Agreements between the leading Underwriter and the Assured are binding on the coinsurers. This applies in particular, in favour of the Assured, to the settlement of claims; the leading Underwriter is, however, not entitled without the consent of the coinsurers – each of whom is to take his decision separately – to

- increase the policy maximum
- include the risks not covered as per Sect. 1.1.2
- alter the currency of the policy
- alter the provisions for notice of cancellation.

In the absence of the consent of the coinsurers, the leading Underwriter is also liable, by virtue of an unrestricted statement of declaration, for the shares of the coinsurers.

9.4.3 In the event of an Underwriter relinquishing the lead, he must immediately notify the coinsurers of this in writing; such notification may also be furnished by the Assured. In such case, each coinsurer is at liberty to cancel the insurance contract by giving four weeks' notice.

The right to give notice of cancellation expires at the end of one month after receipt of the written notification that the leading Underwriter has been replaced.

9.4.4 Statements received by the leading Underwriter shall be deemed to have also been received by the coinsurers.

9.5 **Notice of cancellation**

Notice of cancellation given by Underwriters to the broker shall be deemed to have been notified to the Assured.

9.6 **Relationship to the German General Rules of Marine Insurance (ADS)**

9.6.1 These provisions replace the Special Rules for Insurance on Goods of the ADS (Sect. 80–99).

Unless otherwise provided, they also apply to other insurances covering any interest in or with respect to the goods, for instance to an insurance on anticipated profits or commission or to a special insurance on freight paid independent of delivery.

9.6.2 The remaining provisions of the ADS apply supplemental thereto, insofar as they are not amended by virtue of these Special Conditions for Cargo.

Special Conditions for Open Policies

1 **Basis of Contract**

German General Rules of Marine Insurance, Special Conditions for Cargo (ADS Cargo 1973)

2 **Subject of insurance**

2.1 The insurance covers goods of all kinds or all goods of the class designated in the contract, which the Assured is bound, by virtue of commercial principles, to insure either for his own or for another's account. The insurance does not accordingly cover goods, which the Assured was bound – without legal or economic interest on his part – to insure by special agreement, even if he is specially paid for on this account.

2.2 In an insurance on goods and merchandise of any kind the following goods are, unless specially agreed, excluded:

2.2.1 Precious metals or precious stones, objects made of precious metals or precious stones (excepting industrially utilised products), jewels, pearls, bijouterie, money, coins, securities and works of art;

2.2.2 Radioactive materials and nuclear fuels, insofar as they exceed the legally permissible limits;

2.2.3 Explosive goods as per Sect. 1 a) of the Ordinance on the Carriage of Dangerous Goods by Sea;

2.2.4 Weapons and ammunition (excepting hunting and sporting weapons and ammunition);

2.2.5 Livestock and living plants;

2.2.6 Drugs, to which the currently valid version of the Law on Traffic in Narcotics (Opium Law) of the 10-12-69 applies.

3 **Declaration**

3.1 The Assured is under obligation to immediately declare to Underwriters all shipments and storage under the open policy individually, together with the insurable value. In doing so, he must specify the goods, the type of packing, the means of conveyance and the transport route, indicate loading in containers or oversea vessel lighters and further notify all facts expressly requested by Underwriters.

3.2 In the event of the Assured omitting to make a declaration or making a faulty declaration in respect of the goods, Underwriters are discharged from liability, unless the Assured has not neglected due commerical diligence and has made or rectified such declaration with retrospective effect immediately upon discovery of the ommision or error.

3.3 If the Assured wilfully infringes the obligation to declare, Underwriters are at liberty to cancel the contract of insurance without notice; in such case, Underwriters are entitled to claim the amount of premium which would have been due if the contract had been duly fulfilled up to the time the cancellation became effective.

4 **Goods transhipped and returned**

Goods transhipped and returned are insured on the same conditions as other goods. They must, however, be specially designated upon declaration. The obligation of the Assured to prove that loss or damage sustained occurred on the voyage covered by the insurance remains unaffected.

5 **Duration of insurance**

Insofar as the own insured interest of the Assured is concerned, the risk shall not terminate upon expiry of the 60 days' period as per Sect. 5.2.4 of the Special Conditions for Cargo (ADS Cargo 1973) if, after the goods have been discharged from the oversea vessel at the port of destination, the voyage has been delayed by a peril insured against and the Assured has given notice of such delay immediately. Underwriters shall be entitled to charge an additional premium.

6 **Policy**

6.1 The Assured is deemed to have approved of the terms of the open policy, unless he contests them immediately upon receiving the document. An open policy is not a policy within the meaning of the law and the ADS.

6.2 Underwriters, shall deliver, at the request of the Assured, a document signed by themselves and embodying the declaration for each single transport (single policy, certificate). This single policy is a policy within the meaning of the law and the ADS; the provisions governing approval of the terms of the policy shall, however, not apply to the single policy.

7 **Limits**

7.1 The agreed limits are the maximum sums insured. They apply per means of conveyance and per fire-protected separate store. In the event of the total sum insured of all goods insured under the contract on one means of conveyance or in one fire-protected separate store exceeding the agreed limit, the individual sums insured shall be reduced in such proportion as the limit bears to the total sum insured.

7.2 This provision, however, does not apply where goods have been additionally loaded or stored – beyond the Assured's control – at a port of transhipment, thereby exceeding the agreed limit. Such exceeding of limit must be notified immediately.

8 **Premium due**

The premium is due upon inception of the risk and payable upon delivery of the premium debit note.

9 **Cancellation**

9.1 **Effective upon expiry of the period of insurance**

9.1.1 The contract of insurance shall be renewed automatically for a further year, unless cancelled by one of the parties of the contract giving 3 months' notice prior to expiry of the period of insurance.

9.1.2 In the event of the contract not being cancelled, the latest version of the DTV Clauses on which this contract is based shall apply to the new period of insurance. The text of the new clauses must be notified to the Assured not later than one month prior to expiry of the period of insurance. The Assured shall be entitled to cancel the contract, effective upon expiry of the period of insurance, within 14 days following such notification.

9.2 **Procedure in the event of loss or damage**

Following the occurrence of loss or damage insured against, either party is entitled to cancel the contract. The Assured, however, may do so only if he has notified the loss or damage immediately. Notice of cancellation must be given in writing not later than one month after the payment or rejection of indemnification. The contract terminates one month after notice of cancellation.

9.3 **State of war**

9.3.1 If the open policy also covers the carriage or storage of goods to, from or in a country which is in a state of war or involved in warlike operations, Underwriters are at liberty to cancel that part of the contract of insurance at any time by giving one week's notice.

9.3.2 Within 4 weeks of such cancellation by Underwriters, the Assured is at liberty to cancel the whole contract of insurance by giving one week's notice.

9.4 **Termination of insurance following cancellation**

9.4.1 Where the insurance of goods has attached prior to cancellation taking effect, such insurance shall remain in force until the time provided for termination of the insurance cover.

9.4.2 For goods in storage, excepting intermediate storage in the ordinary course of transit, the insurance shall terminate by virtue of such cancellation on the next declared expiry date, but not later than one month following cancellation.

10 **Insolvency of Underwriters**

In the event of insolvency or impending insolvency of Underwriters, the Assured is entitled to cancel the contract and to insure anew at the expense of Underwriters. Underwriters can prevent the operation of this right by issuing a guarantee.

DTV Strikes Riots and Civil Commotions Clauses 1973

for Insurances governed by the Special Conditions for Cargo (ADS Cargo 1973)

1 **Extent of cover**

1.1 This insurance covers, in accordance with Coverage C (Full Cover), the risks of strikes, lockouts, labour disturbances, political acts of violence, riots and other civil commotions excluded under Sect. 1.1.2.2 ADS Cargo 1973.

1.2 Costs arising from an insured risk causing the vessel not to commence, to interrupt or not to continue the voyage or to call at a port, or causing the goods to be discharged, stored or forwarded by other means of conveyance, to be payable only if recoverable under York Antwerp Rules, 1950.

2 **Cancellation**

2.1 The insurance against the risks as per Sect. 1 may be cancelled by Underwriters at any time provided notice be given two days prior to attachment of the insurance. The insurance of goods in storage – excluding intermediate storage in the ordinary course of transit – may also be cancelled subsequent to attachment of the risk, such cancellation to become effective on the next declared expiry date – but not later than one month – following expiry of the period of notice.

2.2 The notice of cancellation given by the leading Underwriter shall also apply for the co-insurers.

2.3 Legally effective notice of cancellation may also be given by the German Marine Insurance Association (DTV) inserting, for and on behalf of its members, an announcement in the Bundesanzeiger (Federal Gazette). Such notice of cancellation shall be deemed to be received on the day on which the announcement is published in the Bundesanzeiger.

DTV Nuclear Energy Clauses 1973

for the Insurance of the Carriage of Goods – excluding Radioactive Goods or Fissionable Material – governed by the Special Conditions for Cargo (ADS Cargo 1973)

1 **Extent of cover**

1.1 This insurance covers, in accordance with Coverage C (Full Cover), the risks of nuclear energy excluded under Sect. 1.1.2.3, ADS Cargo 1973. Underwriters are not, however, liable insofar as compensation is received by the Assured, or would have been received if this insurance had not been concluded, from third persons on account of the loss or damage sustained.

1.2 Excluded remain the risks arising from experiments with nuclear energy to which the goods may be exposed within a publicly declared restricted area, unless the means of conveyance enters such restricted area without the Assured having any influence thereon. Excluded remain further the risks of war, etc. as per Sect. 1.1.2.1, ADS Cargo 1973.

1.3 Costs arising from an insured risk causing the vessel not to commence, to interrupt or not to continue the voyage or to call at a port, or causing the goods to be discharged, stored or forwarded by other means of conveyance, to be payable only if recoverable as General Average under York Antwerp Rules, 1950.

1.4 Underwriters will indemnify the Assured for expenses only if reasonably incurred or if incurred by virtue of ordinances of the authorities, provided – together

(3) Underwriters are also liable for such loss as results from the necessity to disembark passengers, after an insured accident, in a port of call and, in accordance with legal or contractual provisions, from granting them board and lodging there, furthermore from providing transport other than stipulated in the contract of passage, or from indemnifying passengers for lost or damaged baggage.

Chapter V
Insurance of Disbursements

110. Insurable Value, Measure of Indemnity, Subrogation

(1) The insurable value of claims secured by property exposed to perils of the sea shall be equal to the amount of the claim plus agreed or legal interest and, if the insurance included bottomry or respondentia, also plus the insurance premium for these. If at the time the insurance attaches the value of the property at stake is less than the aggregate claims, then the insurable value shall be equal to the actual value of the property at stake.

(2) Underwriters shall pay the amount insured only in so far as the property serving as a security for the claims should prove insufficient to cover such claims, because it was lost or damaged by an insured peril.

(3) In so far as Underwriters meet a claim they shall be subrogated to all rights and remedies of the Assured. Sections 45 and 46 shall apply accordingly.

111. Measure of Indemnity

Loans on bottomry shall be assumed to be secured by the vessel, the freight, and the cargo; other disbursements by the vessel and the freight.

112. Duration of the Insurance

The cover of bottomry and disbursements attaches at the moment when the Assured has declared himself liable for the money involved. If the Assured himself has paid the disbursements the risk shall attach at the time when such payment was made.

Part Three
Special Agreements (Clauses)

113. "Free from particular Average"

Underwriters are not liable for damage; nor are they liable in cargo insurance if goods are damaged to such extent that they must be considered as lost or destroyed in their original nature. Underwriters are, however, liable for damage that may be due to a sacrifice.

114. "Free from Particular Average unless the Vessel be Stranded"

(1) Underwriters are not liable for damage unless the vessel be stranded. Where it is doubtful whether or not damage is due to stranding it shall be deemed to be caused thereby. Section 113 shall apply accordingly.

(2) There is a case of stranding where a vessel has run aground and can only be brought afloat by extraordinary measures; such extraordinary measures are, among others, the cutting away of masts, the discharge or jettison of cargo, or the waiting for an unusally high tide. The following measures are not to be deemed as extraordinary: the pulling off the vessel with her anchors and the backing of her sails or her screw. There is also a case of stranding if the vessel capsizes, sinks, founders, collides with other vessels or craft, or is fired at, also if fire breaks out or an explosion occurs on board the vessel.

(3) In a cargo policy it is to be deemed a case of stranding where the vessel strikes ground or runs aground or collides with other objects, or if she is damaged by ice; likewise if an event occurs as described in the last sentence of para (2) above. Underwriters are, however, liable only if the hull of the vessel has suffered so heavy damage in the accident that the damage of the cargo may reasonably be attributed to the same event. Failing agreement as to whether fire has been caused by spontaneous combustion, the burden of proof lies with the Assured.

115. "Free from Breakage"

Underwriters are not liable for damage due to breakage. The provisions of section 113 apply accordingly.

116. "Free from Breakage Unless the Vessel be Stranded"

Underwriters are not liable for damage due to breakage unless the vessel be stranded. The provisions of section 114 apply accordingly.

117. "Free from Particular Average under a Certain Percentage"

The provisions of section 34 concerning Underwriters' liability for particular average under three percent of the insured value apply accordingly.

118. "Free from Certain Deductible Percentages"

Unterwriters are liable for particular average only in excess of such percentage of the amount insured as has been stipulated in the policy.

119. "Free from Frustration or Interference by War or Warlike Operations"

Underwriters are discharged from liability where the danger of war begins to interfere with the voyage, particularly if men-of-war, the risk of capture, mines or blockade, endanger the sailing of the vessel, or the continuation of the voyage, or the vessel diviates from her course, or the master is deprived of his freedom of command.

120. "On Safe Arrival", "On Safe Voyage"

(1) The cover ends at the moment when the vessel in her port of destination has cast anchor or has been safely moored at her proper place.

(2) In hull insurance Underwriters are only liable if the vessel, before the time fixed in para (1), has been totally lost or abandoned within the meaning of the provisions in sections 72 or 73, or sold on auction according to section 77.

with other indemnity – they do not exceed 125 % of the sum insured, or if incurred at Underwriters' request.

2 **Limitation of validity**
The insurance does not apply to carriage solely performed on land or inland waterways within Europe or to storage. Intermediate storage in the ordinary course of transit, however, is covered up to a maximum of 30 days; in cases of doubt, loss or damage occurring during such intermediate storage shall be deemed to have occurred during these 30 days.

3 **Measure of indemnity**
3.1 Impairment of usability shall be deemed to be damage.
3.2 In ascertaining the value of the goods in damaged condition, the costs of decontamination necessary for the restoration of the goods shall be taken into consideration, but not expenses solely incurred for protection against any radiation hazard emanating from the goods.

4 **Cancellation**
4.1 The insurance against the risks as per Sect. 1.1 may be cancelled by Underwriters at any time provided notice be given two days prior to attachment of the insurance. The notice of cancellation given by the leading Underwriter shall also apply to the coinsurers.
4.2 Legally effective notice of cancellation may also be given by the German Marine Insurance Association (DTV) inserting, for and on behalf of its members, an announcement in the Bundesanzeiger (Federal Gazette). Such notice of cancellation shall be deemed to be received on the day on which the announcement is published in the Bundesanzeiger.

DTV War Clauses 1977

for the Insurance of Goods carried by Sea and for Air Transports to and from Foreign Countries governed by the Special Conditions for Cargo (ADS Cargo 1973)

1 **Extent of cover**
1.1 This insurance covers, in accordance with Coverage C (Full Cover), the risks of war, civil war or warlike events, as well as events arising – irrespective of a state of war – from the hostile use of engines of war and the presence of engines of war as a consequence of one of these risks, excluded under Sect. 1.1.2.2, ADS Cargo 1973.
1.2 Excluded are the risks of nuclear energy as well as the risks of seizure, deprivation and other acts of authorities based on laws and ordinances in force at the time of commencement of the insurance.

1.3 Costs arising from an insured risk causing the vessel not to commence, to interrupt or not to continue the voyage or to call at a port, or causing the goods to be discharged, stored or forwarded by other means of conveyance, to be payable only if recoverable as General Average under York Antwerp Rules, 1974.

2 Commencement and termination of risk

2.1 The insurance attaches when the goods are on board the oversea vessel or aircraft for the insured voyage, and terminates when the goods have been discharged from the oversea vessel or aircraft and for any undischarged part not later than 15 days after the arrival of the oversea vessel or aircraft at the place of destination.

2.2 If the contract of affreightment is terminated at a place other than the destination named therein, such other place shall be deemed the place of destination. If, however, the goods are subsequently re-shipped to the destination named in the contract of affreightment or to any other destination, such further transit is covered provided notice is given prior to its commencement. The insurance for such further transit attaches when the goods are on board the on-carrying oversea vessel or aircraft for the voyage to the original or other destination. The Underwriter shall be entitled to charge an additional premium. Failure, for reasons beyond the Assured's control, to give the required notice shall not prejudice the insurance for such on-carriage.

2.3 If during the insured voyage the goods are discharged at an intermediate port or other place from the oversea vessel or aircraft, for on-carriage by another oversea vessel or aircraft, the insurance shall be suspended after the expiry of 15 days from the arrival of the oversea vessel or aircraft at the place of discharge; it shall re-attach when the goods are on board the on-carrying oversea vessel or aircraft. During the said period of 15 days, the insurance remains in force after discharge only whilst the goods are at such intermediate port or place of discharge.

2.4 For the purpose of this clause, an oversea vessel shall be deemed to mean a vessel which, while carrying the goods insured, has to perform part of its voyage by sea.

2.5 The period allowed in Sect. 2.1 and 2.3 attaches from midnight on the day of arrival of the oversea vessel or aircraft. An oversea vessel is deemed to have arrived as soon as the vessel is moored, anchored or otherwise secured at a berth or place within the harbour area. If such berth or place is not available there, arrival is deemed to have occurred when the vessel first moors, anchors or otherwise secures within or off the harbour area.

2.6 The insurance against risks arising from the hostile use or presence of mines or floating or submerged torpedoes attaches when the goods are on board a craft for conveyance to the oversea vessel, and ceases to attach when the goods have been discharged at the place of destination from the craft after conveyance from the oversea vessel.

2.7 In the case of postal sendings transported by sea or air, the insurance attaches when the goods are delivered to the Post Offices and ceases when they are delivered by the Post Office to the addressee.

3 **Change of voyage**

Underwriters are entitled to an additional premium if the risks insured against are increased by a change of voyage.

4 **Cancellation**

4.1 Insurance against the risks as per Sect. 1 may be cancelled by Underwriters at any time provided notice be given two days prior to attachment of the insurance. The notice of cancellation given by the leading Underwriter shall also apply for the coinsurers.

4.2 Legally effective notice of cancellation may also be given by the German Marine Insurance Association (DTV) inserting, for and on behalf of its members, an announcement in the Bundesanzeiger (Federal Gazette). Such notice of cancellation shall be deemed to be received on the day on which the announcement is published in the Bundesanzeiger.

DTV Machinery Clause 1973

(Supplementary conditions for the marine insurance of machinery and apparatus)

1 **Insurable Value**

1.1 The insurable value is

1.1.1 In respect of new machinery and apparatus: the ordinary trade value or, in the absence of such value, the total cost of producing the object in its insured construction and imensions,

1.1.2 In respect of used machinery and apparatus: the value as new, in accordance with section 1.1.1,

current at the place of shipment at the time the risk attached, plus the charges for insurance, the expenses incurred up to the time the goods are delivered to the carrier and the freight paid independent of delivery.

1.2 Rebates and price allowances shall not be taken into consideration in calculating the insurable value.

2 **Indemnification**

2.1 In the event of loss of or damage to parts of the goods, Underwriters indemnify the costs necessary at the time the loss or damage is ascertained for replacing or reconditioning the lost or damaged parts, but only in that proportion which the sum insured bears to the insurable value as per section 1 at the time of the assessment of the claim.

2.2 No deduction "new for old" will be made. However, if the value of the whole object is increased by the introduction of a new part, such increase in value will be deducted from the costs incurred.

2.3 The maximum indemnity for any claim, including total loss, is limited to:

2.3.1 The sum insured in respect of new machinery and apparatus,
2.3.2 The current value at place of delivery, or the sum insured if this is lower, in respect of used machinery or apparatus.
2.4 Customs duty and other public dues are not recoverable unless expressly included in the insurance.

3 Particular Exclusions

3.1 Under no circumstances whatsoever shall Underwriters indemnify loss or damage caused by inadequate or improper loading for which the Assured is responsible.
3.2 Breakage of valves or filaments is only recoverable if this is proximately caused by stranding, fire, lightning, explosion or accident involving the means of conveyance.
3.3 Loss or damage occuring when the insured object is being put into operation subsequent to the insured transit is not recoverable, even if such loss or damage is caused by damage occuring during such transit. Claims of any kind for depreciation in value are also excluded, unless the original state of servicability of the insured object cannot be attained by reconditioning.

Instructions to be followed in case of loss or damage

Failure to comply with these Instructions may prejudice any claim under the policy

1. **Inspect goods immediately**
   In no circumstances, except under written protest, give clean receipt where goods are in doubtful condition.
2. **Secure rights of recovery from third parties**
   Shipowners, other carriers, forwarding agents, warehouses, customs and port authorities or other bailees must be
   → requested to attend a joint survey,
   → asked to certify the loss or damage, and
   → held liable in writing,
   where loss or damage is apparent – before taking delivery of the goods,
   where loss or damage is not apparent – immediately upon discovery of said loss or damage.
   Ascertain and observe time limits
   (e. g. for non-apparent damage three days after delivery from ocean vessel, for other damage before taking delivery).
3. Care must be taken to minimize loss or damage and to avert further loss or damage.

4. **Immediately contact the claims survey agent** named in the policy or certificate.
5. **Condition and packing of goods not to be altered** before arrival of the claims survey agent.
6. Immediate notice of claim must be given to Underwriters and to expedite settlement a **full set of claim documents** presented, in particular:
   1) Original policy or certificate of insurance.
   2) Original or copy B/L and/or other contract of carriage.
   3) Original or copy invoices.
   4) Documents showing number, measurements or weight at time of shipping and arrival.
   5) Report of Underwriters' claims survey agent.
   6) Claim Bill.
   7) Correspondence exchanged with carriers and/or other parties regarding their liability for the loss or damage.
   8) Subrogation form in favour of Underwriters signed by the party entitled to the rights out of the contract of carriage.
7. **No claims** can be made on Underwriters if not presented within **15 months** after termination of the insurance.